MAKING THE PLAY

GOLF

BY VALERIE BODDEN

CREATIVE EDUCATION • CREATIVE PAPERBACKS

Published by Creative Education and Creative Paperbacks
P.O. Box 227, Mankato, Minnesota 56002
Creative Education and Creative Paperbacks
are imprints of The Creative Company
www.thecreativecompany.us

Design and production by The Design Lab
Art direction by Rita Marshall
Printed in the United States of America

Photographs by Corbis (Mike Powell), Dreamstime
(Amanaimages, Sergey Galushko), Getty Images (Franklin
Kappa), iStockphoto (t_kimura), Shutterstock (CrackerClips
Stock Media, Fer Gregory, gwycech, magicoven, ostill, studioVin,
Dan Thornberg), Thinkstock (kreinick, Mike Powell)

Library of Congress Cataloging-in-Publication Data
Bodden, Valerie.
Golf / Valerie Bodden.
p. cm. — (Making the play)
Includes index.
Summary: An elementary introduction to the physics involved
in the sport of golf, including scientific concepts such as
torque and lift, and actions such as swinging and twisting.
ISBN 978-1-60818-656-3 (hardcover)
ISBN 978-1-62832-235-4 (pbk)
ISBN 978-1-56660-687-5 (eBook)
1. Golf—Juvenile literature. 2. Physics—Juvenile literature. I. Title.

GV968.B64 2016
796.352—dc23   2015007571

CCSS: RI.1.1, 2, 3, 4, 5, 6, 7; RI.2.1, 2, 3, 5, 6, 7,
10; RI.3.1, 3, 5, 7, 8; RF.2.3, 4; RF.3.3

First Edition HC 9 8 7 6 5 4 3 2 1
First Edition PBK 9 8 7 6 5 4 3 2 1

CONTENTS

GOLF AND SCIENCE

You put your golf club over your shoulder. You swing at the ball on the tee. The ball flies to the green!

Do you think about science when you play golf? Probably not. But you use science anyway. A science called physics (*FIZ-icks*) can help you hit the ball farther. Let's see how!

TORQUE

Your whole body moves to swing a golf club. Your shoulders and hips twist. You lift the club behind your head. Then you swing the club forward.

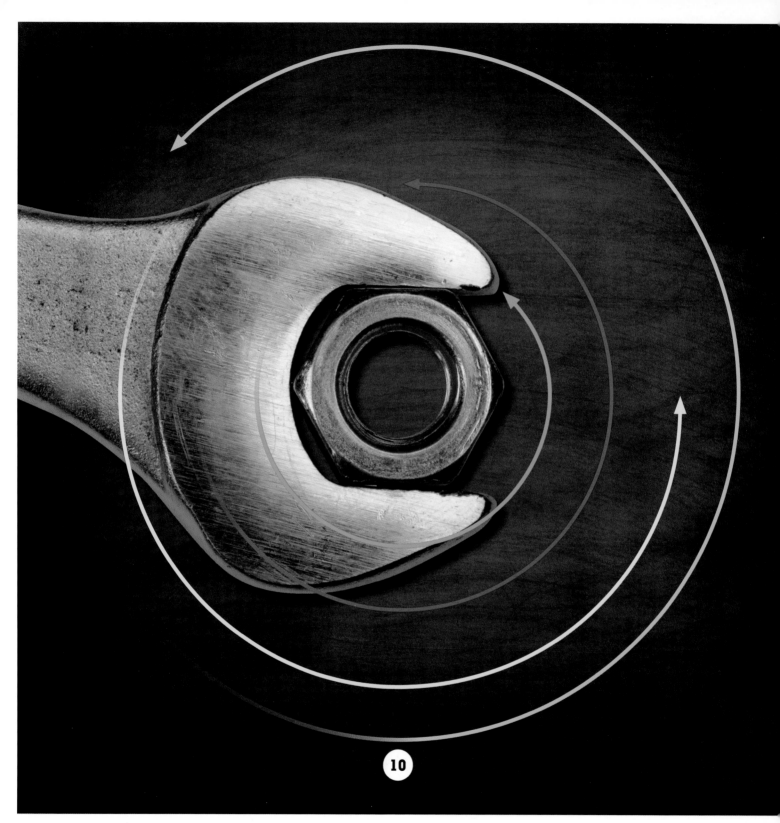

These movements make torque.

Torque is a turning **force**. It is

like a wrench twisting bolts.

The torque of your body is

applied to the club. Torque gives

you a more powerful swing.

TORQUE

A turning force

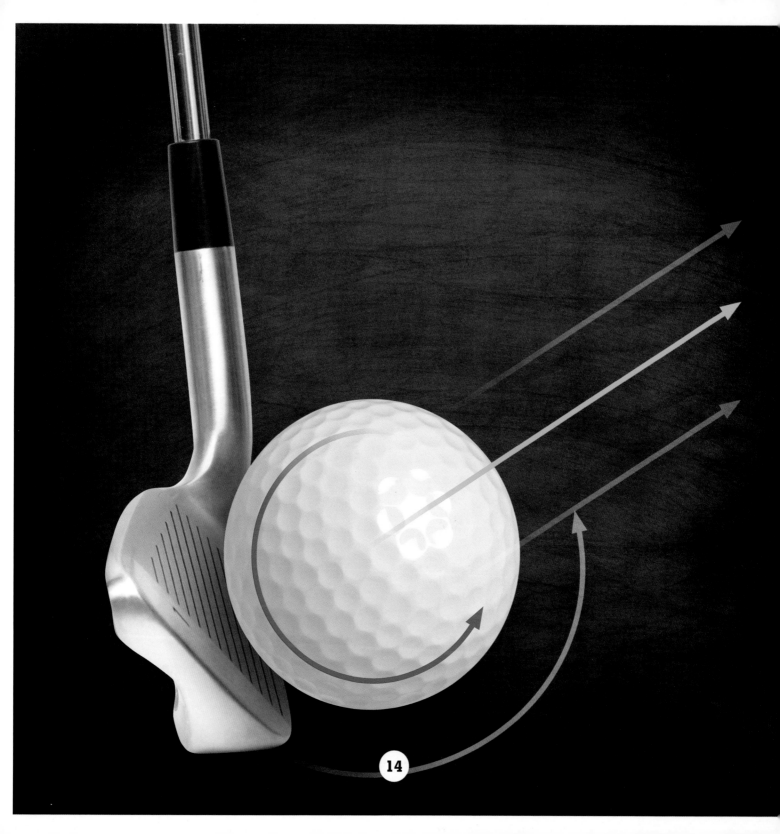

LIFT UP

You hit the ball. It rolls up the face of the club. There is **friction** between the ball and the face. This makes the ball spin backwards. The spin gives the ball **lift**.

15

Many golf clubs have slanted faces. The **angle** of the face affects how much the ball goes up.

How much the ball goes up as it moves forward

LAUNCH ANGLE

17

18

A straighter club face hits the ball low and far. A more slanted face makes the ball go higher. Which club should you use to make a short shot? Give it a try, and make the play!

LAUNCH ANGLES ON THE MOVE

Launch angle affects how high and how far something will fly.

WHAT YOU NEED

- Ruler
- 3 thick books
- Small rubber band

WHAT YOU DO

Place one book on the floor. Lean the ruler against the book so that it makes a ramp. About four inches (10.2 cm) of the ruler should stick out over the top of the book. Place the rubber band on top of the ruler near the floor. Push down on the other end of the ruler. What happens to the rubber band? Repeat these steps with two and then three books. When does the rubber band go farthest? When does it go highest? What does this tell you about launch angles?

GLOSSARY

angle-a measurement of the space between two straight lines that meet at a point

force-a push or a pull

friction-a force that tries to stop two objects that are rubbing together from moving

lift-an upward force

READ MORE

Gifford, Clive. *Golf*. Mankato, Minn.: Sea-to-Sea, 2010.

Gore, Bryson. *Physics*. Mankato, Minn.: Stargazer, 2009.

Walton, Ruth. *Let's Go to the Playground*.
Mankato, Minn.: Sea-to-Sea, 2013.

WEBSITES

NBC Learn: Science of Golf
*http://www.nbclearn.com
/science-of-golf/*
Check out these videos to see where else you can find science in golf.

StudyJams! Force & Motion
*http://studyjams.scholastic.com
/studyjams/jams/science/forces
-and-motion/force-and-motion
.htm*
Learn more about the forces and motions at work in the world.

NOTE: Every effort has been made to ensure that the websites listed above are suitable for children, that they have educational value, and that they contain no inappropriate material. However, because of the nature of the Internet, it is impossible to guarantee that these sites will remain active indefinitely or that their contents will not be altered.

INDEX